Journies in
Continuation

JOURNIES IN
CONTINUATION

AMRIT PAL SINGH

PARTRIDGE
A Penguin Random House Company

To order additional copies of this book, contact
Partridge India
000 800 10062 62
orders.india@partridgepublishing.com

www.partridgepublishing.com/india

CONTENTS

MATE AND MOCK

Minds working
Piecing emotions and words:
Scribbling; typing
Erasing: crumpling: crushing
Emotions awashing:
Sometimes blank, dark
Endless moments of mundane
     Days turn to Days
     Nights into Midnight and Dawn
     Pens silent; Pens Scribbling
     Filling pages: Blanks staring back
     Elation; Exasperation -
     Despondency: Despair
Excitement urges and urges;
Despair weighs heavily:
Wheels and ideas whirl tirelessly
Filling pages;
Idle for stretches consume the
Soul, the Mind - Body;
     Desire to Live and Live:
     Dichotomy leaves one
     Stranded
     At crossroads: At cliffs edge
     Dark abyss stare back
     Fires of blankness consume

Rain of words; expressions consume
Douse
Connectivity lost: Consciousness
Devoid
Blood and Thoughts pulsate.
Enlivening.
Return to the paper furiously
Scribing away;

> Deadlines fast past: Crowds
> surge: Clouding: Ordinaire
> Dull: Putrid: Decandent
> Completion: elation: Singular
> Shimmering: slow: Fragrant
> Compilation: Satiated:

Shemozzle: dishevelled: Unkept
Crushed
Singular solitude beckons mind
And body devoid of, oblivious of
Penning futiristicly: Recognition
Beckons: failure gnaws
Acceptance - Rejection mate and
Mock

> Glitz - Squalor mate and mock
> Egging on shackles to break
> mate and mock
> Cravings and Hunger mate and mock
> Satiation - Fulfillment mate and mock
> Farcical and Reality mate and mock

AMRIT PAL SINGH

Demons and Angels mate and mock
Writer and Publisher mate and mock
Anguish and Joy mate and mock
Night and Day mate and mock
      Meaning of Death and Vacuity
      of Living mate and mock
      Water and Fire mate and mock
      My Paper and My Mind mate
      and mock
I run out of Ideas: Emotions
Who mate and mock

ARE DREAMS WISHES

Are dreams wishes or are wishes dreams.
Do we dream dreams or do dream wishes.
  Do dreams live or do lives dream.
  Do we live dreams or do dreams live
Can we dream dreams or can we wish dreams.
But wishes dream us or do dreams wish us.
  Explanations are dreams or dreams are explanations
  Queries are dreams or dreams are queries.
  But we query dreams or we dream a query
Dreams are answers or answers are dreams.
Do we answer our dreams or do dreams answer us.
  Is love dream or dream a love.
  Do we love dreams or dreams love us.
Is death a dream or dream is a death.
Do we dream death or death dreams us
  Convoluted is dream or dreams are convoluted.
  Do we convolute dreams or do dreams convolute us.
Whispers are dreams or dreams are whispers
Do we dream whispers or whispers dream us
  Silence are dreams or dreams are silence,
  Do we dream silence or silence dreams us
Cacophony are dreams or dreams are cacophony,
Do we dream cacophony or cacophony dreams us
  Dark are dreams or dreams are dark,
  Do we dream dark or dark dreams us.

History is dreams or dreams are history.
Do we dream history or do does history dream us.
      Psychotic are dreams or dreams are psychotic.
      Do we dream psychotic or do dreams do us psychotic.
Pain is dream or dream is a pain.
Do we dream pain or pain dreams us.
      Separation is dream or dream a separation.
      Do we dream separation or separation dreams us.
Hatred is a dream or is dream a hatred.
Do we dream hatred or hatred dreams us.
      That is not what we dream of
      and dream is not that
as a friend of mine says
it's a myriad a kaleidoscope.
Hues are varied
      emotions are varied
      tastes are varied
but wishes are dreams
and dreams are wishes is what it is.

SEARCH YOU MAY

In every moment of mine
        I yearn and search for you
Search for you in your poetic
        Words
Poetic words which I pen
        Try and find and find me
Sometimes in the moments
        Of past, small and fleeting
They maybe
        Maybe in those fleeting
Fleeting moments
        Maybe in you
You
        My existense is there, the
Feeling just slivers past,
        But no: no
I am not there
        Nowhere; nowhere
Do I exist
        I am not there;
In your thoughts
        In your fragrance;
In your dreams;
        In your sights

AMRIT PAL SINGH

Yes; yes nowhere I am
        Definitely not there
Nowhere close or distant
        There is no place no nook
Nook where I search
        You may search
Search you may
        Or I may search
May I search

YOUR TYME

She came you asking your

Atteyntion

You sais you were busi

She called you in the middel

Of the nigh

You sais you want to sleeps

She fout with you fore no reason

Juss to spend

Soom time talking to the ones she

Neids the most

You sais shes impossibul

Yas shes baid, demanding

Possesiv, jalous, weak,

Emoytionul, yas she throws

A lot of tantroms rite

But; butt remembar

Onse upon a tyme when you; you

Wer alon

Yay luked at the Moon and sais

I'll give everything for someone

Who disturbb me all the tyme

She donts want any big gifts

Or choclates,

Wat she wants is josut one Hugg

From you

No matther how many tymes she
Sais she loves you
She juost wants to listen I love you
From yoer side
Little fights don't matther for you
But yoer every little thing
Upsetts her like Hells
She cant forgets easili,
She is plain possessives
She doesn't want; doesn't want
Waunt to loose you
She doesn't waunt Monies,
Gifts choclates or
Or any uther
What she wunts
Wunts is your Tyme
You broke her heart and; and
the stranger part is dat
she still loves you

UNEXPLAINED HOW :;

Unexplained; unexplained
A dream unexplained
A reality unexplained
        I chase the beats: beats of
        Of my heart; slow so slow
Racing: racing away
Tearing: tearing
        Ripping: ripping away moments:
        Moments: times: eons passing;-
Passing away; ticking away
Ever so slowly
        Pulling me: me closer - closer
        To you
Telling: whispering I want: want
To spend my life with you
        Future clouds; clouds my vision
        Emotes pull and tug away
Away all my senses; my sanity
Desires longings fill me
        Fears grip me on visions of loneliness
        Vice like they encompass me
Wishes: wished: wish that
I am close - close to you
        Eternity of togetherness; oneness
        Togetherness; oneness

Closeness - closeness beckons
Yanks and beckons me
    Sorrow, ecstacy, companionship
    Isolation: myriad of sentiments
Emote me
Gather around me
    Wishes - dwams of simpatico
    Hold me: bind me: plod me on
Rails of life bound by sleepers
Visions;dreams;wishes hold me And you
    Taking us together on this
    This journey into sunset
Bound we are: together for eternity
Separation: thoughts of severance
    Haunt, gnaw at my core
    My core; my being
How can we change: do we change
Or is it a way of life
    Our togetherness has filled me
    Completed me
Emotions, joy, sorrow, everything
Just: just seem to gallop
    Gallop away in my dreams
    Wishes and my life
Unexplained are the ways of
The heart: the heart, mind and soul
    Like a wild rampaging beast: like the wind
    They run away: blow away
Eyes of yours burn away all
The demons, all the emotions

An empty calm prevades
Soothing, emotionless: swept away
Lullabyes, songs, words are chocked
Chocked in my throat
Soul stirring they are, humming
Away deep, deep inside
Lifting, reaching a Maestro's
Cresendo
Applauding: heroics of my soul
Heroics of my love
Togetherness beckons, loneliness
Tediously fades away
Complete I am or am I complete
Emptiness seems to wish away
Complex is the way
Complex is the query;
Complex is the riddle
Complex is the solution the answer
But I know that;
That you are and always were
The one who completes me
Unexplained how:;

Fires of passion

Amazing; amazing it feels to be in love
In love with you:
So free, like a bird
A bird just relented
Relented from cudgels
> Soaring; soaring
> Paradise of your arms
> Beckons my flights of fancy
> Homing to your love
Warmth you radiate;
Warmth I gather from you
Warmth and peace
I get no matter where I am
> Love you always
> I bleed for you always
> My Angel you are
> Angel of my salvation
> You are
Yonder: I may go
Close I maybe
See you I may
See you not I may
Love you forever I will
> Love of you
> Passions fill me

Words may run out
Feelings will never
Never satiate
Passions overflowing
Fires of passion still burn
Stoking my heart: my mind: soul
Unending Love

Breaths I have to take back

Tread slowly,
Slowly do pass my Life
Debts: debts do I have:
Have to repay
Debts of someone –
Debts to you
Life: debts to you
      Some pains I have
      Have to wash away
      A few promises to keep
      A few honours to honour
      Keeping pace: pace with you
I have tread on toes:
Left behind somethings; someone
Placate I have to someone
Bring a smile to someone I;
I have to
      A few dreams: dreams
      Desires unfulfilled are
      Some undone chores;
      Chores remain undone
      Desires hidden
      Hidden and secreted
      To be washed away
      To be buried they are

Relationships made; some broken
Some slipped away
Some let go
Wounds; wounds of these fester
Wounds have to be healed
     You; you will move:
     Move on; move ahead
     But wait I want to;
     Wait I want to:-
Ironic that; that
I can live without you;
The breaths I take are dedicated;
Dedicated to someone;
Breaths I have to take back
That I have to tell someone

God We Forget

Blue planet beckons me;
Beckons me to sit;
Sit with her:
Share with her
Confide in her
Laugh with her
Sob with her
      Because this;
      This is where we belong;
      Rivers have taught me,
      Streams have taught me;
      Oceans have taught me
      Lakes have taught me:
Taught me life'
Taught me how to live
      Silently tread
      Tread silently in wake;
      Wake of my concience;
Change 'change I
I want; want to but;
But my desires:
My desires, my avarice;
Desires avarices and
And pangs of hunger

Fuel me; fuel me
Fuel me like I never knew
Onward onward I push - push
Push to quench, quench
Quench greed quench avarice
Pleasure I myself, pleasure myself
Myself I do,
Exotic is what I want
Want exotic is what I desire
Cars, clothes, houses,
Bejewelled watches; watches bejewelled
Rare and antique
Antique and rare
Capture timeless, time
Time I want to capture
Ticked away time; time ticked away
Waits not for me, for me it waits not
Waits naught for the rare, the antique
Taught and preach we are Purity
Purity; purity of heart
We talk of and teach
Preach of heart; purity of heart
Avarice and desires
Lying in the convoluted mind
Mind convoluted
Plays tricks on me
Tricks it plays on me
Torn I am
I am torn

Mind or heart
Heart or mind
This was not; not this was
This was not told
This was not preached
This was not taught
The mirror we seek
Mention we do
Yearn we do
Of loved ones
Moments elapsed
But God
God we forget
Forget God we do

Infinite; Love

Amazing; amazed feels
Feels to love in be
Feels; feelings;so
So light feeling so free
Soaring like; like
Dove

    Dove like; dove like
    Released; released
    In the sky;
    In the sky

Soaring; soaring
Flights;
Released from cages
Cages; cages
All the cages

    Arms yours hold me
    Hold me; hold me
    Paradise; paradise
    I know none other

Home; home is
Is your love
Love of yours is;
Is my home;

    Warm: warmth
    Warmth; exudes

Exudes forth from;
From your love
Peaceful; serenity
Serenity envelopes; envelopes
Envelops me; far
Far or near I maybe
Angelic; angelic
Angelic you are; Angel
Angel of mine;
Mine Angel you are
Wide and far I may;
May I go; go away
Far and further; further
Love; love you I will always
Passions; passionayte
Passionayte your love;
Love drives; drives me
Kindling my life
Vocabulary; idioms; words
Words; dry up; dry up
Describe Love of; of you
Your Love I cannot describe
Endless; enduring
Feelings overflowing; overflowing
Passion; passionayte
Consumed I am by Love
Your love; love consumes
Consumes me:
Infinite; Love; love
For you is such

DOLOROUS STAR I AM

Feeling friendless, forlorn
Deserted star I wander in space
Desolate star I shine for light
Destitute star I am search family I do
Empty star hollow I am
Homeless star I shine on finding home
Isolated star I am solitude engulfs
Lonesome star I am singular in existence
Reclusive star I am friendless I wander
Solitary star shine I alone
>   Abandoned star I am exorcised
>   Alone star I am make my own galaxy
>   Apart star I am my is different in hue
>   By oneself star I am unique I am
>   Comfortless star I am no one I lend a shoulder
>   Companionless star I am ostracized
>   Disconsolate star I am tears I shed
Down star I am as guide no one I do
Estranged star I am as forsaken I am
Godforsaken star I am as God left me
Outcast star I am as rejected I was
Renounced star I am as secluded I stand
>   Single star I am as unattended I orbit
>   Unbefriended star I am as uncherished I am by peer
>   Unsocial star I am as withdrawn I am within me

Abandoned star I am as companionless I am

Deserted star I am as desolate I roam

Detached star I am as forlon I remain

Friendless star I am as hermit like I live

In solitary star I am as isolated I wander

Lone star I am as lonely it is

Lonesome star I am as I have me and my shadow

Single star I am as sole I am

Solitary star I am as solo I exist

Travelling light star I am as unaccompanied I sail

Unaided star I am as unassisted I am

Unattached star I am as unattended is my galaxy

Unescorted star I am as unmarried I plod widowed

Bleak star I am as black I radiate

Cheerless star I am as comfortless is my aura

Dark star I am as discouraging I speak

Dismal star I am as dreary is my life

Gloomy star I am as hard and harsh is my orbit

Hopeless star I am as joyless is my existence

Lonely star I am as melancholy and mournful is my tenor

Oppressive star I am as oppressive is my persona

Sad star I am as somber is my façade

Desert star I am as arid is existence

Bare star I am as desolate infertile sands cover me

Solitary star I am as uninhabited is my soil

Unproductive star I am as untilled I remain

Waste star I am as wild one I am

Deserted star I am as bare I wear

Barren star I am as bereft of nutrient of love

Derelict star I am as desolate it is

Empty star I am as forlon is everything
Forsaken star I am as isolated and left I was
Left in the lurch left stranded star I am as galaxy moved away
Lorn star I am as neglected I feel
Neglected star I am as relinquished everything I did
Solitary star I am as uncouth is my breath
Uninhabitated star I am as vacant are my spaces
Destroyed star I am as dreary is I
Empty star I am as lonesome and ruined I am
Unfrequented star I am as unoccupied and vacant I lie
Disconsolate star I am as bereft of light bleak and black I am
Forlon star I am as dismal and down cast I wake up
Companionless star I am as dejected I sleep
Inconsolable star I am as hurting I am forever
Dolorous star I am as joyless I grow
Lonesome star I am as miserable my existence is
Somber star I am as tragic and wretched it is

PONDER

Ponder; as I ponder over my morning
Coffee
This beautiful sunrise adumbrates me
Times; the times I have spent with you
    Times; the times I couldn't spend with you
    Glued; how we stuck to each other
    Like glue
    Distant; how distant we were separated
    From each other
Appraise; appraise about my future
Thank; I thank you for making my
Life richer
Moments; the moments with you
    Moment; the moment I opened my eyes
    Think; I thought about your smile
    Missing; was missing you all this while
    Just; just like your pretty face
So just smile and grace
Days; the day; days ahead
Ponder; ponder I every moment

Steely metal edifices

Shimmering lights
Glassed over eyes
Dull metal edifices
Extension of limbs
    Extensions of mind
    Extensions of souls
    Extensions of thoughts
Greed - avarice combine
Extending far beyond
Far; far beyond
    Limbs – Mind – Soul – Thoughts
    Unmindful in their
    Endeavours; dull
Dull metal edifices
    Slice – Stab – Slash – Silence
    Splatter; Flesh
    Flesh; Bone; Sinew
Unmindful; unmindful silently
Stealthly, grabbing life
Life; snuffing it out
    Instantaneously – grudgingly
    Perilously; pathetically
    Gruesome gory outcomes
    Over vanquished
The steely metal edifices

Lord and prevail
      Dreams vanquished
      Desires vanquished
      Eyes vanquished
      Minds vanquished
Gardens vanquished
Homes vanquished
Relations vanquished
Glories vanquished
      Life vanquished
      Master of vanquished
Perils and miles covered
Covered to conquer
      Minds and souls doused;
      Doused to conquer
      Wealth and health combined;
      Combined to conquer;
Righteousness and wrongness combined;
Combined to conquer;
Greed and lust together;
Together to conquer
      Opportunity and Avarice taken;
      Taken to conquer
Amidst I stand;
Screaming;- screeching
Scratching; Crying; Hoarse
      Helpless at this Cowardice;
      Shattering my existence
      Shattering my existense
Shattering my Being

Shattering my Soul; my Mind
Shattering my Comfort
>   Shattered I drift along
>   Strewn leaves; strewn Bones
>   Strewn Blood; Strewn Souls

Winds – water take me away
Wading – Floating
>   A medium to another
>   Watching Steely metal edifices
>   Start the cycle Again

PEACE

Peace courses my heart, and blows
Through me like a zeypher
Peace courses me like a fragrance
Peace courses me like rays
Peace tears asunder noise and worries
Peace seethes through my quietude
Please like a globe of fire, expands fills my
Omnipresence
Peace like an ocean, rolls all in space
Peace like red blood, vitalizes veins of my
Thoughts
Peace like a boundless auerole, encircles my
Body of infinity
Peace flames blow through the pores of my
Flesh, and through all of space
The perfume of peace flows over the gardens
Of blossoms
The wine of peace runs perpetually through the
Wine press of all hearts
Peace is the breath of stones, stars and sages
Peace is the ambrosial wine of spirits flowing
From the cask of silence
Which I quaff with my countless mouths of atoms

No More Than Friends

Down memory lanes, growing up together days to months to years
Somewhere I lost track and remembered beginnings of meeting
pulsating beginnings
breaths shortened, constrictions
captured to look into your eyes

Looks of your at me
Smiles so radiant, eyes radiating warmth
Gazes, smiles, warmth were not for me
Realization I knew this could never be
Pools of despair I drowned in
I stared through those vacuous eyes
Dawned on me, I will never be loved

Entomb, enshroud my feelings
Friendship remains just friends
that was how it was going to end
I knew just how you felt
I could feel it burning inside
That the love we shared could never be
No more than friends,
which is exactly how it began..

MY LIPS ARE SEALED

My lips are sealed
This feeling for you, I must confess
My heart rapidly beating inside my chest

Thoughts of you have filled my day
Fumbled words I struggle to say

Shaking quietly from deep within me
Filled with desire for what might be
Standing here silent, waiting to speak
Wave of fever have redden my cheeks

So much to say not a word was spoken
Lost my thoughts, my voice is broken
Silence is heard, my words are amiss
Nothing uttered, my lips sealed a kiss

Eyes Windows

The eyes windows of the heart
Where-in emotes dwell
A myriad feelings
From where tears do flow.

Eyes say contents of heart
Speech two lovers speak,
Silence eloquently starts
Romance muted communique.

Orbs of windows of cares,
Display sad and wearied soul;
Distant looks and empty stares
Reveal a man not whole.

Feeble attempts conceal
Clearly felt and seen-
Showcase all the stuff inside
Deep secrets where love was.

Windows of kindness
Caressing looks embracing,
Blessing words of forgiveness
Bitter hurts spews forth, tears.

AMRIT PAL SINGH

Eyes Love open windows,
Joy, happiness; twinkle
Forthright dancing
Goodness, flowing.

PASSING THROUGH

Clouds pass by the expansiveness.
Somewhere in me I melt into the cloud,
shapes hues shifting wafting,
twisting churning mingling.
expanses covered wind blown
sails of dreams wet mud smells
I can't breathe.
gushing puffing billowing air around.
twisted intertwined heavy dark,
wispy tongues cottony, streaks,
devilish look of their eyes.
threatening, teasing playful,
annoyed, calmly they
saunter my body, my soul.
days end, night beckons silent vigil
Anyone around??
screams, wishes floating as they spew
light dark a game they play
dry drought wet floods a game they play
shamans dancing to their muse
music dance they bring with angels
melody in the pitter patter of the raindrops
they conjure
dreams and puddles with muddles
on the cloudy boat

these ride,
wafting through reality and dreams
Oh, now I understand.
Their music is too loud.
YOU cannot hear me.
Reveling and gloating,
YOU are too full of your own life. ?
I fight my battle.
reality and make believe
footloose.

Cold Memories

Sitting all clad
Winter days and night upon
Chattering teeth
Dying embers long gone
Gone cold memories
Memories long cold
Gazing at long minutes
Gazing at long hours
Grudgingly pass on
On the grime covered dial
Passing times bringing no cheer
Passing times bringing shiver
Passing breaths cloud up
Cloud up disappear
Hanging droplets add
Add the cold
Warmth desired
Desired dearly
Times chimes knells
Knells sounding
Muffs covering
Covering desperately
Desperately shutting out
Shutting out knells
Chimes and times

Whistling winds
Trembling leaves
Heavy snows cover
Covers not thrown away
Shivers the trees do
Barks cover life
Leaves shiver die fall
Piling up
Covering blanketing
Blanketing ground
Deathly silence of sleeping
Sleeping hibernating
Beings hidden
Hidden behind earth
Earth filled caves
Snow laden panes
Loneliness pervades consuming
Sanctuary of the comforter
Sanctuary of my loved
Beckon tide over
Tide over the loneliness
Tide over the winter nights
Tide over the journies

WHISPERS

Whispers whispering breezes
Hints hinting of showers
Kiss kisses of the clouds
Anticipation premonition of thunder
Merging melting together hues
Greys blues rainbows
Dark and light
Pall gloomy, bright cheerful
Scents smells wafting
Parched, wet earth
Billows bending branches
Water filled drops
Drenching
Greens turn greener
Hues more bright
Air fragrant with
With myriads of smell
Memories dreams float
On whispy dark clouds
Traversing expanses; eons
Traversing make believe reality
Whiffs - déjà vu
Bliss unfolds forth
Monsoon mania abounds

BLOSSOMS SPREAD

Battered, broken,
Dreams; lives; wrecked,
Soul devoid body.
Desire to live trill,
blossoms spread fragrance around.
      Soul Scarred, began to run.
      every breath was a task.
      Layers of grime, dirt, rebuke
      cover the soul.
blossoms spread fragrance around.
      Oppression, tribulations heaped
      hapless and weak.
      no compunction in violating.
      Everything said, anathema.
blossoms spread fragrance around.
      I look within, I have to rise,
      or I will remain fallen.
      I have to dig deep,
      to bring out the tenor in my voice,
      from the depths of despair.
blossoms spread fragrance around.

      spring in my step,
      confidence and grace.
      truth, Without doubt and hesitation.

My life mine, my creation.
blossoms spread fragrance around.
I rise from my ashes.
soared, my existence.
Life meaning, unfettered, unchained,
live my dreams.
blossoms spread fragrance around.
adversity, heartache, conquered
express my desires.
bitterness unlocked,
strife made me stronger.
blossoms spread fragrance around.
Walk with poise and grace.
No longer hurt
Truth my companion,
everything is ME.
blossoms spread fragrance around.

Awaiting homecomings

Memories pacing through
Reality dreams piece together
Reason; Sense come together
Words jumbled garbled jangle,
Jangling keys heavy in noise
Passing times they make me realise
Songs; Notes fill the vaccum
Fuel; Fire the moments gone by
Glory; Sun filled moments
Gone so soon
Motion; Wind fill the sails
Sails of time pull away
Wharfs I not Own; Wealth neither
Sails of time tug away
Lamp; Light tell of days past
Fast they change Day; Night
Impressions of feet in Sands
Drumming of sounds bellow in shells
Reminds of clutching sands passing fingers
Faded pictures strung in frames,
Running length of Cold Hallways,
Unsung songs unremembered notes;
Un memorized Faces of multitudes:
Déjà vu belongings unknown,
Autumn leaves colder sunsets

Reflection of lined faces mirror,
Mirror faded color hair time
Jangle in times well spent
Tirelessly turning windmills,
Churning memories tirelessly fill the mind
Trudging so reluctantly away:
Away from the womb of the sea and beaches
Waves calling out, Setting Sun whistling
Sounds wafting over Shoulders,
Eternal playing out the Same notes,
Varied hues adding flavours,
Awaiting homecomings

Emotes serene and meditative

Grievieng cries

Gripping heart wrenching

Peels of laughter

Warm encompassing

Warming the cockerels

The heart

Reminiscent of passed

Passed away souls

Souls restitution

Water nourishing souls lives

Embraces the winds

Shimmering silver lites

Lites up the very beings

Lulling one asleep

Guardian angels tread along

Tread guarding

Encouraging endearments whispered

Paths of life

Paths of life becoming easier

Acceptable to accept failings

Loneliness vanishes, vanishes

Guardian Angels companions

Companions they become

Bonhomie cradles they bring

Sojourns no longer

Fear no more vice like grips
Unfetered mind churns out
Uncomplicated verses
Coursing over pages
Coursing over words
Coursing over phrases
Emotes not existing forth out
Emotes smite the times
Emotes reach out
Emotes drench the eyes
Emotes wrench the heart
Emotes play riddles in my mind
Emotes serene and meditative
Emotes encase encapsulate ensnare
Emotes ensure exact mystic ethereal
Emotes run gallop envelope the love
Emotes ensnare words wishes
Emotes entangles binds grief
Emotes entangle bond love

SANDS, MOMENTS

Sands of time
Winds of time
Ticking of time
Memories of time
Fading of memories
Tests of time
Companions of time
Friends of time
Enemies of time
Times spent on time
Moments spent on time
Little glances of time
Meeting deadlines of tome
Ghosts of time
Smiles of time
Twinkling of time
Guffaws of time
Smirks of time
Values of time
Wastes of time
Hearts of time
Pining of time
Glances of time
Shyness of time
Tongue tied of time

Opportunities of time

Elapses of time

Dresses of time

Make up of time

Missed opportunities of time

Brightness of time

Darkness of time

Love of time

Spite of time

Acceptance of time

Rejection of time

Value of time

Nonchalance of time

Reverence of time

Oneness of time

Separation of time

Joys of time

Anguish of time

Holding of time

Slipping away of time

Obscurity of time

Oblivious of time

Wishing of time

Wishing away of time

Obscured by time

I was then

Obscured by time

I am now

Relevant by time

I was not then

Relevant by time
I am not nowadays
Sands of time
Sands of memories
Cloud my obscurity
Cloud my existence
Stand alone
Lonely, clutching at
Sands, moments

THESE CLOAKS SHIELDS

Tugging tugging at cores

Cores

Stretching stretching times

Minutes months year

Year Elapsed

Traversing strenuous times

Times imprinting changes

Departing away

Au - courant unspoiled sparkled

Sparkle neoteric minutes months year

Laced tinges lingering

Lingering savouring conge'

Dread deceive greet;detest

Wary yearning beckons au - courant

Dread dread springs of fester

Festering despairs gnaws gnaws

Nibbling away remnants of sanity; purity

Shield shielding them them we

Lumber on lumber on furtive glances

In obscurity we desire to dwell

Shroud them them we cloak away try

Try to cloak

Nature shines shines

Thawing thawing away shields and cloak that

Cloak that we cling to

Cloak that we cling to
Constant constant is the gaze
Constant is the thaw
Dark crevices of soul and mind we
Mind we conjour up to cloak
Souls we encompass encompass
Simple simple thrust us egging
Egging us forward,
Thrusting us in the shine
Thrusting us in the thaw
Cloaks and shields renounce
Souls egging us renounce shields and cloaks
Deep dark crevices fill up
Fill up with these
These cloaks shields
Burdens we lug around
Burdens our crosses to bear
Burdens we rid; ridden free
We are goaded to tread

SINGULARITY DESIRED

Daggers rapiers falchions
Scimitar toledo cutlas
Anlance bodkin poniard
Skean stylet machete
Scythe sickle skiver
Strewn around they lay
Complete killing she did
She kills with disarming
Charm aplomd dexterity
She can kill with a smile
Wounds gashes slashes
She does
Lacerate tendons stifle breaths
Anguish she can cause
Tug away a heart beat
Tug away a breath
All she needs is a smile
A smile to smite
Lacerate torment grieve
Chastise harrow
Calumniate aspersions guile villification
Play with your resolve
Resolve dissolved facades broken
whispers in the winds
faint distant catch phrases

fleeting reveals glimpses enthralling
exhibits so exquisite alas hidden
hidden as fast
secrets driven into the bosom
exciting puzzles to be unraveled
onward into labyrinths
labyrinths emotions beckon
uncharted nameless paths roads
taken ridden travelled
truth
bastions of lust; lust
obscure reason; ransoms of
desires burn paid off
rejection bastions compel you
mocking clouding intents
reasons of sanity
run away whirls of insensitivity
whirls of insecurity
rising dust storms hiding
love endearments
sanity hath no meaning
sanity rejected
deceit plunders scything away
veracity actuality a mere figment
truth lies blur
merge converge distant move away
dancing death dance
clarity sanity driven away joint
inebriated mind inebriated soul
sensuality creating illusions

the construct remains hidden
edificing alone accumulating
enduring all
niches carved
roots deepened in
ready to weather the vagaries
paths well tread some untread
readiness surprises thrown up
challenges head on taken
singularity desired
singularity achieved
vanquished odds lay strewn
amongst
Daggers rapiers falchions
Scimitar toledo cutlas
Anlance bodkin poniard
Skean stylet machete
Scythe sickle skiver
Shines she does

ILLUSIONS CLOUD REASONS

Motoring the unending expanses

Fixed on the black

Black metal line constructed

Clarity beckons

Opportunities I seek

Prospects I pursue quest

Inspiration ardor I want to reach out to

Calamities left behind

Torments vexation all bundled up behind

Bright frolic filled days

Miracle comfort fortune dazzle

Glint glinting in mirrors

Aglow limpid lustrous

Ahead pristine primordial

Mirrors of nature ahead

Mirrors man made

Reflections of souls

Changes and some the same

Clichés

Ironies

Reflections semblances illusions

Views come in flashes

Mirrors man made conjour

Visions in my mirror the sun is going down

sinking behind; behind me

Bridges; bridges in the road
I; i envision of all the good things
that we; we
Conscious have left undone
and i agonise worriment
profess cynicism
of the butchery; butchery to come
the senescent fetters gives way
Confusion runs rampant
Nature and man play games
and suddenly it's day again
the sun is in the east
even though the day is done
Conjourer works of art
Games played; fictional; reality
Lines division merging
Mirages delusions semblances
two suns in the sunset
illusions cloud reasons
Utopia existence threatens
could be the human race is run
impending doom looms
the relisation before
the assassin pulls the trigger
and you slide towards life and death
stretched stretched the frozen moments with your fear
voices unheard
faces unseen
touches untouched
vaccum and stillness of nothingness

prevails control no more
reality dawns
fears evaporate
leaving only charcoal to defend
finally i understand
the feelings of the few
ashes and diamonds
foe and friend
we were all equal in the end

"THE NIGHT MUTATES"

Imperceptibly by sporadically
the night mutates around
Mutates around.
Leaving moving on
In its wake dreams
Desires avarice
Greed debauchery
Mellow moonlight
Star filled skies
Cuddles loved ones gave
Mutated lights bright
Dews shimmers
Winds warms
Counting the leaves
Which tremble at dawn
Rays piercing assuaging
flowers colourful opening
lean on each other in yearning
cornices rest the the sparrows
humming birds
flowers
insects worms
awaken
driven to the heart of the sun.
acclivity prominence seek

watches watching dawn

silence pervades its loft

steely resolved steadfast

mutates watching

spectator

dances light shadow

watching silent

ovation forthcoming neigh

shadows shimmer soothing

lights linger

wisps clouds

cosmic spectacle dance

danced

spaciousness epochs traversed

creator creation all entwined

mystic mystifying

incandesce incinerate scald

day mutates

mutates around

shimmery silky smooth

soothing awash

piercing darkness

invocate imploration veneration

heaven way

aping the mutate

giving noth

grabbing salivating

egoistical narcissistic

parades of aplomb

garish spectacle parade

halos construct sequestered
forbidding haughty incurious
inebriated revelry
delirious cocky
heading to the
the amore
the mutate
the sun

"Ways and Means"

Fortune greenbacks I collect,
run, rush, pillar to post, maddening traffic
Multitude papers I fill; greenbacks I desire
Unending questions,
 situations; answers
Get a good job with more fortunes
and the world approves.
Money, it's a high addict, a habit
Grab that cash with avarice hands,
New car, caviar, seven star daydreams,

Money runs away, groping left after
I'm all right, till you keep your hands off of my stack.
Money, it's a hit, red carpet glitter
blood bone gore I take to get it
No do that goody good bullshit
join I have the hob-nobbinng first class traveling set
Lear jet, dazzling cars, yatches
I grab glittering watches
Time I try catch - like greenbacks

Money, a crime I commit
stash it I will hoard it I will
Smell it wear it spend it splurge it
All that is evil

Never part it share it ever
Snatch it I will grab it I will
Cheat for it, thieve for it, kill for it
Charity it but for own gain

Beg for it, ask for it always
Divide it never, wager for it
Loan for it, barter for it every time
Part with it no one does
Earn it, labour for it, sweat for it
They say, toil for it, save for it
But no one gives it away.

I was in the right!"
Yes, absolutely in the right
certainly was in the right
greenbacks is what I want
Steal, cheat, grab,
Stash it, bribe it, gamble it
Smell it, spend it, splurge it
Always everytime

Solitude beckons.

Singular, disconsolate
Grasping, clutching at wind
Desperately seeking to catch
Clouds, rainbows, moonlight
Thoughts, dreams, words
Perceptions, touches, aroma, closeness
Oneness
Chasing – chasing happiness
Stumbling, laboring, perspiring
Blurred lines euphoria failure
Hell fires heavens serenity
Pains gnawing blessed blue skys
Living pulsating fields of green
Cold dead-lines miles steel rails
Smirks smiles dissimilar yet so similar
Mirages reality lies truth blurred
Trade - offs spin - offs acceding conceding
Ghosts illusions tomfoolery delusions
Hallucinations chimeras,
Heroes personage
Abstrused, cloistraled obscured
Burnt out stumps stare back
Greenery devoid smoldering remains
Blistering scorching glares
Wafts cools unseen

Horizons blind filled heat stare
Heats cages wars heat and cools
Loneliness clouds reasons
Loneliness messes dreams
Loneliness muddles emotions
Loneliness stabs sounds
Loneliness kills murders
Years tick away
Tugging away semblances
Omnipresent loneliness presents
Solitude fears pangs grip vice like
Roads roads traversed
Similar dissimilar
Likeness crazes
Depression, despondency defeat
Drum the dredge, doom looms
Solitude beckons deafening
Souls wrenched drenched
Solitude encompasses

LONELY; I WALKED

Lonely
Lonely I came,
Cared for
Cared by
Caring for
Lonely; I walked
Walked
Corridors of classes
Corridors of loneliness
Lonely; I walked
Stares of peers
Stares of seniors
Stares; stern
Stern stares of
Teachers
Rebukes; rebukes
Peers, corypheus
Shower; awash
I awash lonely
Lonely;
Lonely I morph
Rebukes, implosions,
Triumph, adversity, depths
Despair I handle
Lonely,

Loneliness, imperfections, despondency

Consternation

Handle, endure

Lonely

Pillars, seas, expanses

I cover, climb

Lonely I remained

Lonely

Lonely I passed away

Lonely; lonely

I trek expanses

STRUTS

Climbing

Climbing; struts

Struts

Prop me up

Struts

Support me; strengthen me

Struts

Fatigue me; weaken me

Struts

Slip me; grip me

Struts

Grasp me; hold me

Struts

Unshackle me; dissuade me

Struts

Shackle me; comfort me

Struts

Horizon me;moonlight me

Struts

Heights I climb; depths I fall

Struts

Elate me; despond me

Struts

Hunger me; feed me

Struts

Choke me; breathe me

Struts

Defeat me, glorify me

Struts

Grow me, stunt me

Struts lonely

Lonely they leave me

Struts surround

Surround me cloister me

Struts breathe

Breathe me making me live

Struts defeat

Defeat me work again, start again I do

Struts companion me

Companion me in my desires

Struts complete me

Complete me in my journey

Eons awaited

Serenity
Wafts through
The waves of soul
Singularity I seek
Singular my soul
Singular it seeks
Serenity soul seeks
Callings I fail
I fail
Fail to understand
Gay abandon
Beckons
Callings of home
Aromas of culture
Tugs at every sinew
Mates awaited
Singularity pangs
Pounds
Deafening feverish
Pulverize lacerate
Souls shredded
Sanity insanity
Singularity annihilated
Monotony want to
To break

Paused
Are the eons
Paused
Eons awaited
Creations
Wonderous admired

LONELINESS TALKS TO ME

Grassy knolls'
Trolls,
Grassy paths,
Grassy meadows
Grassy pastures
I walk on
Walk to many more,
Gaze upon,
Wonderous of awe,
Awe I see,
I see what I cant
Cant replicate
Pebbles, stones,
Rocks,
I see not,
Mosses, grass,
Mildew,
Dandelions
Cover my
Smooth paths,
Meander, I
Meander
Paths I find
Paths I choose
Paths some find me,

Paths some seek me,
Grassy paths,
I choose,
Wide, cushy;
I seek;
Stumble I not:
Strumming;
Humming;
Dreaming,
Wanton;
Gay abandon;
Singular,
Humming;
Dreaming,
Wanton,
Gay abandon;
Singular: Loneliness;
Accompanies me
Loneliness my symphony;
Loneliness my sonnet;
Loneliness my companion;
Loneliness,
Loneliness
Talks to me

Years – years have drifted away

Watches, clocks; pendulums sundials; Ticking away
Houres dayes momentes completeing
Dull, wastefule, insipid, walk awaye dayes,
Lyeing, vacante, closede, mindes numb
Unimaginative, breathese in out, daed much daed
Lights dim, blinke cursors stares; stares
Just just; disgust; stagnation ponderous, dug in
Dug in oure gravese, gravese of dull insipid
Cover us; tombstonese, marking our existence
Counterpane welcomes; welcomes dull insipid
Countinge sun rayes, rayes, dropes dropes of raine
Watching watching, dancing duste; duste particles
Longe; longe life is what we thinke we haveth,
Killeth time theth why we do today
Killeth; killeth ticking - ticking away the tymes
Laeft laeft behind; laeft behind in the race
Paneting paneting; striving sprinting
Trying; trying catche catche houres,
Tyme tyme moving moveing catches
Catches againe againe - moveing ahead againe
Slippinge, slippinge away, sandes sandes of tyme
Sun is there there; celeste celeste is there
But I; I am no longer younger; no longer younger
Drumming heart; pulsating veins; breathes breathes
Short, short; gasping, clutching clutching.

Grasp; grasp I cannot the wind,

Grasp; grasp I cannot the tyme,

Grasp; grasp I cannot the dreams,

Grasp; grasp I cannot the sands,

Slippede, slippede, away graspes empty

Pages empty, ink potes empty, pens empty

Mindes empty, thoughts empty; fingers

Fingers twiddling empty air they type

Tyme, tyme, halve empty ink pot, halve empty

Halve empty paper, but a daye, a monthe,

Years – years have drifted away

Monk monk like I staye at; staye at

Home; home cocoon; cocoon;

Comfort; comfort I seek; my escape

My escape; my prison; my fiefdom

Tyme tyme stand still; the waye I want

The waye I desire; the waye I think

My temple; my convent; my hermitage

My pilgrimage; my cavern;

My magic land

Uncomfortable

Greetings I greet,
Minds in bodies are you there?
Illusions I see, whispers I hear.
Is there anyone, any soul?

Perceive you, feel you
Voices I hear, low and whimpers
Panaceas, I bring, I carry:
Enliven you, I Endeavour

Breathe easy, simmer down
Want to hear about your pains, fears
Ears I am to all your ramblings
Aches, wounds, scabs where it hurts?

Pains lingering, throbbing, are receding
Distant ships, distant memories, dimming on the horizon
Your and my pains only coming through in waves
Lips moving I can't hear what you're saying
Palpating, numbing, spasms of pain awash
Bound, gagged, tethered to fences
Willing to break free, float; float in the skies
I can't explain, comprehend can't you
This is not how I am

Calm; remain calm
Probe; Just a little probing
Just jogging your memories!
Stirring the pot; delving into you

Made you sick? Can you stand up?
Can the real you satnd up? I see you; the real you
Uncomfortable I made you
Uncomfortable with yourself
Uncomfortable with what you have become
Uncomfortable to sit through my show

I caught a fleeting glimpse
Of the Child you were; The Dream that you dreamed
The mirror is clouded now; the memories clouded
Uncomfortable; uncomfortable we are
Uncomfortable with what we shaped
Uncomfortable with what we achieved
Come on, it's time to go.

IDOL

Remember MJ, Remember Bee Gees
when you; we were young,
times; moments shone like the sun.
Shining in flares, oil slick hair
Broad Buckles; Rhinestoned jackets
Crazy diamonds.
Vinyls, Walkman's precious
Coloured TV's a fantasy;
Shady 8mm; Tabooed Beer
A stolen puff; stolen corners and nooks
Crazed a look in your eyes, black holes
Shiny idol lost; lost to the world

Caught in the crossfire
Childhood lost and starry dreams,
Smithereens blown on the steely breeze;
Steely breeze of reality
A target for ridicule
Stranger you have become
No longer the known
Ignomity becomes you stranger,
Idoltary lost not your legend, abrade and polish!

Blazes, passions, You reached too soon, we yearned for the moon.
Too much too soon, the idol soon faded.

Shadowy at night, and exposed in the light.
Idols flaws shone through
Visions, teeny worships willed you.
Diminished you wore out your pedestal
Random; precision, eroded on the steel breeze of time.
Rise you inamorata, you graven,
You prime mover, and shine!
Nobody knows where you are,
Once again be the Idol.
Remove Layer after together the bricks around.
Once again be the Idol..
And we'll luxuriate in the blaze of yesterday jubilance,
Once again be the Idol.

MY ENEMY AND ME

Lines formed, Legions ready
Phalanxes ready, My enemy and Me,
Forward; forward

Cries I hear cries from everywhere
Who knows what we would predestine to do
after all we're only ordinary men

Clashing steels and the front rank died
Thee General pondered, we as the lines on the map
Swayed as sashaying satin dresses
Pink and Blue; Divine dreams of gossamer;

Steel points razor sharp stab and pierce;
And life and death stare and
neither my enemy or me ever
knows which is which and who is who

Fast and furious Up and Down
Death played;Lines; dots on Maps we are;
Macabre dance Death life;
Victory defeat

And in the end it's dots, Lines, insignificant
Blotches to be wiped;
or to wipe other blotches

Macabre; emotes devoid
Cruelty; vicious; Chilling

Lines, inches; yards; acres; Divide us
We fight for;
sitting across tables; sitting across maps
Haven't you heard it's a battle of words

The Standard bearer cried;
Listen my son, Stabbed, clubbed; impaled;
There's choices for you inside the Legion; the Phalanx

"Well, they're going to kill you,
if you give them; your choice; your life
short, sharp death, They will do it again.

Drunk, heady your Blood and Gore causes
Causes a Stupor, Addiction for;
sitting across tables; sitting across maps.
It's only the difference between Legion and Phalanx
manners of death cost nothing do they?"

Down and Out we crawl
It can't be helped With, without
And who'll deny that's what the fighting's all about

Get out of the way, it's my Life on the anvil
And I've got things on my mind
For want of the price of dot or a line
The Blood and Gore flows.

YONDER THE HORIZON
THE PLACE WE LIVED

Yonder the horizon the place we lived
when we grew up
In a world of simplicity and miracles
Our thoughts worked constantly and without boundary
Time ringing constantly

Down the Long Road on the Changes
Do we still meet the simplicity and miracles
Jagged memories followed our footsteps
Scurrying before time took our dreams away
Forsaking the myriad that tied us to the Yonder
A life consumed by senescence

Yonder; The grass was greener
Yonder; The light was brighter
Yonder; With friends
Yonder; The nights of wonder

Smoldering burnt out bridges beckoned
Glimpses of Yonder green on the other side
Sleepwalking back; Steps taken forwards
Inner emotes Dragging with flag unfurled
Dizzy heights of a dreamy world

Shackles of desire and ambition
Lingering hunger still unsatisfied
Dead weary eyes still scrutinise the horizon
Oft walked turns, obstacles this road we've so many times travelled

Yonder grass was greener
Yonder light was brighter
Yonder tastes were sweeter
Yonder nights of wonder
Yonder friends surround
Yonder dawn mist glowing
Yonder water flowing
Endless; Forever and ever

Fatal attraction

Into the distance, bandarole of black
Drawn out to the point of no turning back
Flights of fantasy covering a windswept field
Standing alone impressions reeling
Fatal attraction stead fast,
How can I escape this irresistible grasp?

Wandering visions waver to and from the expanses above
Icicles gather around me slowly surely
uncharted desolate, all knowing I thought,
Windjammer nowhere; clutching at whisps of clouds
Unladen, empty disappearing in fists
Freedom of flight beckons, with a lump in the soul,
Leaden, icicle laden, rooted; wish to fly

Winging the azure skies fantasies and prayers,
Desire's of a Halo, vanish in the expanses,
Icicles Across on my fantasy wings reflect shadows
Shams of reality, stark, bright, blind me
Dreams undreamed wakened by the morning light
Night dawns and brings no mollification;
There's no sensation to compare with this
Suspended animation, a state of bliss

Sovereigns Awaited

Guttural; ghoulish throaty voices

Wailings; whimpering pleas

Animalistic adrenalin running

Hounds frenzied flesh devouring awaiting

Dogs of war and men of despise

Death, taking a life, sovereigns awaited

Sovereigns collected aforehand

With no cause, nothing or no one to discriminate

Adrenalin death driving

Peace, harmony enemies despised

Religion, culture unvalued

Treasures looted; stashed away

Sovereigns traded for ills of the flesh

Satanic sins frought sought enjoyed

Irrelevant sides; glittering gold

Crispy crackling minted notes

Sides we turncoats are

Piles of bodies pools of blood

Our currency;

flesh and bone takers; grim reapers

Hell opened up and put on sale

Hootch, rotgut sponge up we Gather 'round

haggle hard cash, we will lie and deceive

Weak eared we seek out; gutting contracts made

The Grimreaper and Even our masters

Know not the web we weave

A battleground it's One world, it's

One world, and we will smash it down

Dogs of war and men of despise

Will smash it down

Invisible killers; tillers of death fields

Reapers of sovereigns; brokers of transfers,

Whispered long distance calls,

Hollow deathly laughter

Hatred spewing words over winds of voices

In marble halls, in taverns, in jungles

Deserts, mountains we disdain,

Wheels, machines munitions; Butchers

Moved, Steps have been taken, a silent uproar

Silently; stealthily; Avarice has unleashed

the dogs of war

Machinations You can't stop;

you can't stop what has moved

invisibly;

Not Signed, not sealed, oblivion looms large

Unleashing a dark side, to say the least

And gambling in death is the nature of the beast

Dogs of war and men of despise won't negotiate

Dogs of war and men of despise don't capitulate,

Dogs of war and men of despise and the meek will give,

And you must die so that the grim reapers will live

Dogs of war and men of despise will grow

No matter how many are scythed

Killing fields, hatred spewing words

Avarice driven

Will flourish more
But wherever whenever you go,
They know they've been there before
Death winners cannot lose
Whatever is changed,
Dogs of war and men of despise remain.

ACROSS A WEARY ROOM

Restless wandering eye
Scorn laden, contemptuous views
Across a weary room
Dull, dark nooks, uncleaned
Debauchery dripping filled
The atmosphere
Immersed in my own evils
Ills covered, cloaked me
 On the highway to hell
on the road to ruin
Self ruination I drove everyday
speakers garishly coughing out
Irrelevant tunes
No heed paid to ribald lyrics
Reeking of innuendo
Morality on the wane, chastity
Chastity vanished with the night
Dance no longer dance
An erotic writhing induced
Induced by avarice reeking out
Out of the atmosphere
Temptress I engaged; engaged
Erotically; erotic The music played
Played as we twirled without end
Thrusting; pulsating demonic

Provocative, egging towards shameless

No insinuation, no solicitation

Honour blown away eons ago

None of it to defend

Imposed my will,

The temptress resigned to my request

with a toss of the mane

My resolve stretched to the test

Strangulated propriety; immersed;

Immersed in desire, libido on fire

Fires of the pyre beckoned

Reckless; reckless

Cautions and consequences

Not a worry

Decadence overpowered

Slithering; writhing

Falling into the vortex;

Vortex of libido

Cascading; drowning; choking

Abyss; hells fires singing

Putrid smells of burning desires;

Burning fleshes

Flash of a moment

Tying a dying life to a dead life

Ruefulness no more forgotten

Carnal ravenousness; lechery

Exhilarant, provocative

Pleasures of the flesh

Sliding, swallowed in the cavern

A blink of the eye

sinking into the flesh
Carnivorous a life for life
Regretful not; remorseful not
Elixirs of poison coursing
Elixirs of decadence all consuming
Peace eludes and vice awakens
Awakens all consuming
Flames a fire of vice engulf
Satiate pleasures of flesh
Unending; cyclic; diabolical
Machinations working plotting
Seeking the hidden guilty
Fitting pleasures of flesh
Fitting plotting minds like a glove
Sanity eluded; senses numbed
Moments slipped by
Seeds of debauchery sown
Poisonous pleasures to be reaped
Taking no time at all

Roam aimlessly

Averting, the glassy looks
Creepy, crawly sensations
Contemptuous looks
Kingdom threatened; kingdom
Of privacy; a metal box on wheels
Cringing as they roam;
Roam aimlessly
Despising raspy voices
Cacophony of blaring and raspy
Attempts to block; cast away
Phrases – words incomprehensible
Reaching out; out to us
Guttural raspy the;
The uncouth and
And the downtrodden\
Invading; invading
Our commodious existence
Tribulations of the uncouth
Uncouth – Downtrodden
Gibberish, incomprehensible
Unacceptable, invading
Oblivious of suffering
Sufferings piled on
Day after day
Hour after hour

Emotions turned dead

Emotions bordering the dead

Unacceptable, unknown

Willingly shunned to accept

Growing dissent, growing multitude

Teeming numbers

Shadows lengthening

Shrouding cloaking out the

The light

How long can we

Can we shun away the multitude

How long can we

Carry on with leaden hearts

How long can we

Cringe at their sight

How long can we

Cut out the guttural cries

How long can we

Cannon fodder the uncouth

How long can we

Crumble the downtrodden

How long can we

Cripple the crutches

How long can we

Clutch to our crutches

How long can we

Cold shoulder the smoldering

How long can we

Castigate the ideas of the unsung

How long can we

Cocoon from the environment around
Staring; staring at the proceedings
Shunning out what we don't want to
Want to accept; want to ignore even
Even when its stench is around us
Covering us, surrounding us, shrouding us
Shrouding our light; shrouding our intellect
Unmindful of our own suffering
Unmindful we are what we are
What we are becoming
Dreams over; reality
Reality painfully
Painfully rips at sensibilities
Awakening to the darkness
Awakening to say good bye to sunshine
Awakening to loneliness of utopian
Surrounded by strange goings on
Winds of change mesmerized
Flames lit but coldness encompasses

Mindful of the second step

Begin and start to close in
Mindful of the second step
Or the next and the next
The first step is what counts
That's what starts
It's the step one doesn't want to take

Ground Beneath, firm comforting
Steps we can take on
Sure footed I am on it;
Akin to the conversation I start
With the question I ask
With the comment I want
Snub the others
Impose your will on the conversation
Rough shod all around

In order to hear
Hear someone else's voice
Tune into and follow
Your own voice
Wait; wait
Until you hear that voice

Wait until; until
One develops
Develops into an intimate
Private listener
Patience beckons to hear
Tune attune to another
Another pitch
Another voice

Carving a niche; a niche
Of your own;
None to follow, but your own
Rally to no one's false; false
Bravados; false calls of war
Credos follow; of own
Others not to emulate
But; but listen and adapt

Begin and start to close in
Mindful of the second step
Or the next and the next
The first step is what counts
That's what starts
Journies

How does one write

How does one write
Write for someone else
A poet; a writer
Admired; accolade
Demised; demised
Debated upon so long
Answers oft not known
Buried with the pages
Pages penned, printed
Yellowed aged
Read and re read
I wonder; wonder
How I will take steps
Steps of my own
Ideas I can pen
Pen of my own accord
Crutches, clutch at straws
Verbs, adjectives desert me
Nouns and adverbs a distant memory
Knitting, weaving sewing
Words blurred
Humble, insignificant in
In presence of the Creator
Yearn for recognition
Voices reverberating with my

My given name
Warmth of the voice
Which calls out my name
My lost nouns, verbs,
Adverbs, adjectives, commas
Collected, close to my bosom
Unknown, unrecognized, unheralded
Distribute it how; where do I
I pour them out
Unknown books, unknown hordes
Accept them will anyone

Wade into battle I do
Armed, clothed with, shielding me
Words, questions, answers
Blows of ears, thrusts of tongues
Raipiers of wisdoms, I flail,
Words, questions, answers
My unknown lost nouns, verbs
Blunt some, glancing blows wisen me

Battles fought, lost some, won some
Firmly footed I am
Woven into the fabric of speech
Woven into the necklace of words
Woven into the tapestry of books
Myriad hues welcomed
Existence justification; justified;

Twiddling thumbs

Twiddling thumbs; scribing
Furiously on the glass pane
Glass pane of my companion
My companion of all time
A life time consumed
Consumed gazing; wonderous
Raptures awaited
Amazement; amusement
Pensive, erotic addiction
Possessive, passionate
Passionately I pour in my;
My soul, my time;
Extension of my being
My alter ego; or I am its alter ego
Flames of passion engulf me
Passion of its possession
Passes away the bountiful;
The bountiful, the plentiful,
Surrounding me,
Sunlight I no longer desire
The dim glow emanating warms me'
Moonlight I despise;
Flashlight I admire,
Colours varied; changing I abhor
Mega pixels I boast

Minds and conversations no longer invigorate
Giga bytes is my craving
Do I need to climb the mountains
To visit the holy vistas
All by my self?
What to do?
What is my work?
Where is my home?
Who are my people?
Where do I belong?
Where am I needed?
Simplistic; minimal a connect;
Connect with the bountiful
Elusive but within grasp
The sharp tinge of chill in the morning
Jolts the sleep out; widens the eyes
Freshly bathed Earth welcomes you
A companion less shared

WHARFS

Well nigh Midnight
The houses asleep
Sleep their dreams
Enclosed in them
Tales of ships, of Clocks passed
Of Houses daily proceedings
Mundane
Tales of Voyages
Salt filled waves rolled
Wharfs docked safely
Steps confidentently taken
Pride in Crew swells chest
Embraces of Families so desired
Houses; Homes returned to
One after the another
Rows and rows
Down cobbled stones
Lined along
Walls supporting each
Leaning to support
Breathing as one
Standing apart some
Willing to become one
One of the multitude
Dark, Light windows stare

Stare out to cobbled stones
Large windows frame the facades
Some smaller dot the facades
Draped some drawn drapes
Reflecting dances of routine
Some crowded some singular
Loud, melancholic, life filled
Breathing living like one
Driveways some empty
Some catching the mist
Hearths warm
Beds warm beckoning sleeps
Beckoning dreams

Warming Souls

Paces I take
Brisk with purpose
Cane an accoutrement
Bench at the turn awaits
October air the evening
Breathe, breathe in the
Coolness different it fills
Fills the lungs
Hint of a breeze
Rustles the leaves
Dried as they fall from
Hues blue brown red white
Ditches fill in with
Onto on or off trees
Dew or mist wet them
I need not knoweth
But somehow you and i
Meet in the rain
Puddles on the doorway we form
Walk in from the rain
When we do;
Ham sandwich we have
Coffee to wash it down
Telephone each other

Late alert evesdroppers wary of
Moment to moment pass
Stringing lanterns of words
Lighting fireflies warming souls

Blinded bounded oxen trudge

Blinded bounded oxen
Trudging paths well trodden
Circles unending traversed
Merriment tunes of bells strung
Clinical clockwork sounds
Sounds buckets filling emptying
Splashing regularly steady
Steady stream passing
Parched tongues waiting
Rejuvenation awaited
Parched lands waiting
Parched plants waiting breakthrough
Sickles awaiting ripening
Dullness precedes rasping
Rasping ripened harvests
Grains awaiting mill stones
Greenbacks awaited
Crushing grinding powdering
Hunger beckons gnawing
Consuming souls bodies characters
Devouring lands souls bodies characters
Delirious avenues lit
With chandelier souls
Of infusoria
Rising from Pharoah's tombs

White sky light
Of lunar lusts
Ecstatic dust and ashes whirl
Hallucinatory citadels broken
Conquered
Shattered souls through shattered glass
Peers darkness pools whirls
Whirls of unending ecstacy
Flocks of dreams blow around
Shores afar oval oceans beckon
Immortality time wrap desired
Skies breached eyelids blank lights
Lights sounds bombard
Waxing waning waves euphoria
Constant euphoria needles
Blinded bounded oxen trudge

Journies In Continuation

Journies afresh

Journies anew

Jornies refreshed

Some journies in continuation

Some journies breached

Journies broken

Journies constructed

Some journies reconstructed

Journies some taken over

Taken over trodded paths

Some journies revisited

Some journies revived

Journies some taken in

In memory lane

Some journies quaint

Some journies jovial

Journies some taken

Taken down the aisle

Journies taken over sacrament

Journies taken to wedding bells

Journies taken joyous

Journies taken heart rendering

Journies taken union families

Some journies taken tugging at heart

Some journies taken to betrothal

Journies taking away our jewel
Taking away our heart our life
Journies of new beginnings
Journies taken of joy
Journies taken of lifetimes
Some journies I travelled to join
Some journies I travelled to mend
Some journies travelled to reverence
Some journies traversed taxing
Some journies of freeness I travelled
Some journies of repentance taken
Some journies of reconciliation I have taken
Journies of fledgeling steps turned
Turned to strides
Strides taking journies unknown
Journies with circumspect I take
Journies with renewed confidence I take
Journies with a twist taken
Some journies meander aimless
Intrigue mystifying journies some
Justifiable some unwarranted journies some
Hurried harried journies taken
Wanton gay abandon some times journies
Childlike playful enticing journies
Crest fallen depths of despair hapless journies
Vacuity desolation compounded journies
Dark caliginous sunless some journies
Fathomless profound soliquoy some journies I take
Ebullient flippant exultant journies some I walk
Winter moons summer moons journies cover

Frosty glacial journies I meander

Coruscating flaming scalding flaming journies I wander

Journies every waking moment

Journies every day every month

Journies done some undone some incomplete

Journies controlled, spiraling out of control

Nectarous unsavoury journies I take

Edacious esurient rapacious predatory journies

Sated saturated contented gratifying journies

Journies, journies complete me complete my life

Printed in the United States
By Bookmasters